I Wonder Why

Vultures Are Bald

and Other Questions About Birds

Amanda O'Neill

KING*f*ISHER

NEW YORK

KINGFISHER
Larousse Kingfisher Chambers Inc.
95 Madison Avenue
New York, New York 10016

First published in 1997
10 9 8 7 6 5 4 3 2
Copyright © Kingfisher Publications Plc 1997

LIBRARY OF CONGRESS CATALOGING-IN-PUBLICATION DATA
O'Neill, Amanda.
    I wonder why vultures are bald, and other questions about birds /
Amanda O'Neill.—1st American ed.
        p.   cm.—(I wonder why)
    Includes index.
    Summary: Answers such questions about birds as why a parakeet
cocks its head, which bird likes to wade in the mud, and whose nest
has heating.
    1. Birds—Miscellaneous—Juvenile literature.   [1. Birds—
Miscellanea.   2. Questions and answers.]   I. Title. II. Series: I
wonder why (New York, N.Y.)
QL676.2.066 1997
598—dc21 97-188 CIP AC

ISBN 0-7534-5093-3
Printed in China

Series editor: Clare Oliver
Series designer: David West Children's Books
Consultant: Michael Chinery
Illustrator: all cartoons Tony Kenyon
    (B.L. Kearley)

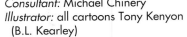

CONTENTS

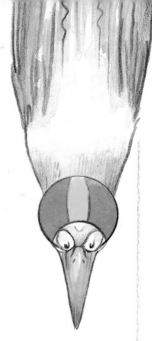

Which bird is a giant?

The ostrich is the biggest living bird. From top to toe it's over 8 feet tall—that's about as high as the ceiling!
And it's heavy, too, weighing about the same as a Shetland pony!

● The biggest flying bird is the wandering albatross. From wingtip to wingtip it's as long as a car!

● The ostrich can't fly. But it can run from danger at up to 45 miles per hour—that's faster than a racehorse.

Ostrich

Which bird flies fastest?

Eider duck

The eider duck can fly along at up to 65 miles per hour. But the real record-breaker is the peregrine falcon. It swoops down on its prey at over 125 miles per hour, making it the fastest animal on Earth.

Peregrine falcon

● The fastest swimmer is the gentoo penguin. It can race through the water at up to 17 miles per hour—that's three times faster than the fastest person.

Which is the smallest bird?

● The African kori bustard is the heaviest flying bird. Sometimes it even has trouble getting off the ground!

In tropical rain forests, many of the birds are smaller than the butterflies. The Cuban bee hummingbird is probably the smallest of all. It's about as big as the eye of an ostrich—and can perch on the end of a pencil.

5

Why are birds special?

Birds are not the only animals with wings, the only ones that lay eggs, or the only ones with beaks. But they are the only creatures in the whole wide world that have feathers.

● Birds aren't the only animals that fly. Bats do, too—and they're mammals.

● Birds aren't the only animals that have a beak. The duck-billed platypus does, too.

● Birds aren't the only animals that lay eggs. Tortoises and other reptiles do, too.

- All birds have wings, but not all of them can fly. Some creep, hop, or run along the ground; others swim like seals in the sea.

- There are 30 birds in the world for every man, woman, and child.

Which birds have scales?

All of them! Birds' feet and legs are covered with scaly skin, just like the skin of snakes and lizards. That's why you never see birds wearing shoes and socks! But the scales don't stop there. A bird's feathers may seem soft to touch, but they're made of tough, horny stuff—just like scales.

Why do birds fly?

Flying is a great way to escape from enemies. With a few flaps of its wings, a bird can get to a safe perch well out of the reach of a hungry cat! Being able to fly also helps birds to move quickly from one feeding ground to another, and to catch insects that zoom through the air.

● The handsome roller bird is a true acrobat. When chasing insects, it performs somersaults in the air.

How do birds fly?

The normal way for a bird to fly is to flap its wings up and down. This pushes it through the air, just as oars push a rowboat through the water. But it's hard work, so some birds save energy by gliding. Once they've built up speed, they spread their wings out and let breezy air currents carry them along.

● Like planes, birds need to be strong but light. To keep their weight down, they have hollow or paper-thin bones.

● Hummingbirds are the only birds that can fly backward. They can also fly forward, sideways and upside-down!

● The common swift spends nearly its whole life in the air. It even sleeps on the wing!

How many feathers does a bird have?

The bigger a bird is, the more feathers it has. A hummingbird has about 900 feathers, while a swan has 25,000! Feathers come in all different shapes and sizes. Soft, downy feathers keep the bird warm, others keep it waterproof in the rain, and the strongest feathers give it the power to fly.

● Birds have long tail feathers, smooth wing and body feathers, and fluffy down feathers. Down is warmer than fur—it's like a bird's thermal underwear.

Tail feathers

Golden pheasant

Pheasant

Body feathers

Parrot

African gray parrot

Goose

Scarlet macaw

Guinea fowl

Down feathers

● Every wing feather is made up of hundreds of hairlike strands. These zip together with tiny hooks to make a smooth, strong blade.

Why are vultures bald?

Vultures are messy eaters. They feed on dead animals, pushing their heads right inside the bodies to tear into the meat. If they had head feathers, they'd get dirty and sticky, and would be almost impossible to clean. That's why vultures are much better off being bald.

● Feathers work so hard that they wear out. The bird grows a new set each year and the old ones gradually fall out. This is called molting.

Wing feathers

Parrot

Seagull

Macaw

Flamingo

Turkey

Quill pen

● Before pens were invented, people wrote with quills. These were large feathers, usually from geese or swans, sharpened at the end and dipped in ink.

Who eats with ...giant tweezers?

A hungry toucan pushes leaves apart with its big, long beak. Then the bird uses the tip of its beak very delicately, like tweezers, to pick fruit off the branch. Next it tosses the fruit up in the air and snaps it up as it falls.

● The Galápagos woodpecker finch is the only bird to use a fork! It grasps a twig in its beak to poke out insects from holes in the trees.

...a pair of pliers?

● The sword-billed hummingbird's beak is longer than its body. The bird uses its beak like a straw to suck nectar from deep inside a flower.

Crossbills feed on the seeds inside of pinecones, and they have a very special beak for prying them out. The top half of the beak twists over the bottom half. This helps the birds get a good grip and force the cones open.

...a strainer?

The inside of a flamingo's beak acts like a strainer. Hairlike "combs" along its beak strain out water, mud, and sand from the mouthfuls of tiny water creatures it scoops up.

● The frigate bird is a real pirate. When other seabirds catch fish, it attacks them, and steals their booty!

...a spear?

The anhinga is a waterbird that feeds on frogs and fish. It stands stock-still in the water for hours, waiting for some dinner to swim by. When it spies a catch, it spears its prey as quick as a flash with its long, dagger-like beak.

● The secretary bird of Africa hunts with its feet! It catches snakes in its claws and stamps them to death.

Which is the biggest eagle?

The harpy eagle is bigger than a Great Dane, and is the largest and most powerful of the eagles. It lives in the rain forests of South America, where it chases monkeys through the trees, grabbing them with its deadly claws!

● An eagle's feet are deadly weapons. Its toes are strong enough to crush its prey, and its claws are razor-sharp.

● Some birds are experts at fishing. When an osprey dives into the water, it can catch and carry off fish more than half its own size.

• Vultures sometimes eat so much that they can't take off after their meal.

Which birds have sneaky wings?

Most owls hunt at night, swooping down silently on rabbits, mice, and other tasty prey. These hunters have special fringed wing feathers, which can beat the air without making a sound. That way, their prey doesn't hear them coming, and has no time to escape!

• The Everglade kite lives on water snails. Its hooked beak is just the right shape to pry a snail from its shell.

• Owls eat their prey whole. Later, they cough up all the bones and fur in a neat little sausage-shaped pellet.

Why does a parakeet cock its head?

A parakeet's eyes are on the side of its head so that it can see all around. But seeing things close up is harder work. The bird has to cock its head and aim a special viewer in the middle of its eye—a bit like when you aim your camera to take a picture.

● The woodcock has the most extraordinary eyes. Without moving its head, it can see what's going on in front, behind, and even above.

Which bird steers with its ears?

The South American oilbird makes its nest deep in a cave. It can't see in the darkness so, as it flies, the oilbird makes nonstop clicking noises, which echo when they bounce off the cave walls. By listening to where the echoes come from, the oilbird knows exactly where the cave walls are.

● Ducks have a pair of see-through eyelids that protect their eyes when they dive. The eyelids are just like swimming goggles, helping ducks to see under water.

Which bird sniffs all night?

The New Zealand kiwi hunts at night, using its nose to sniff out worms, insects, and other tasty tidbits. Unlike other birds' nostrils, a kiwi's are at the end of its long beak. To find itself some dinner, all it has to do is stick its beak into the soil and sniff around!

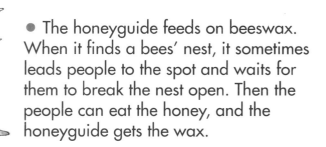

● The honeyguide feeds on beeswax. When it finds a bees' nest, it sometimes leads people to the spot and waits for them to break the nest open. Then the people can eat the honey, and the honeyguide gets the wax.

Who's the best-dressed bird?

Male birds of paradise grow beautiful lacy feathers during the breeding season. When a female comes by, all the males hang upside-down to show off their stunning plumage. It's a beauty contest, and the female picks the bird with the finest feathers to be her mate!

Do all birds sing?

Just over half of all birds sing, but the rest are far from silent. Geese honk, owls hoot, seagulls mew, and the kookaburra seems to laugh. It's mostly male birds that sing—to attract a mate or to warn other males to stay out of their territory.

● In some New York houses, parrots are trained as burglar alarms! They let out piercing shrieks if someone breaks in.

● The male palm cockatoo attracts a mate by playing her a tune. He grasps a twig in one foot and uses it as a drumstick to beat a hollow log.

Which bird looks frightening?

If you scare a hawk-eagle, it'll probably scare you back! This bird has a crest of long feathers on its head. When it feels threatened, these feathers stand on end. This makes the eagle look bigger and fiercer than it really is—with any luck, it will frighten away any enemies.

Which is the smartest builder?

The male weaverbird has to prove he's a good nest-builder before he can win a mate. He hangs from a branch, weaving long strips of grass into a hollow ball. If his nest is good enough, the female will line it with feathers. If not, he has to start all over again!

● Many birds spend the night huddled together in sheltered spots. This is called roosting, and it helps them to keep warm, especially in winter.

Which nest has heating?

The Australian mallee fowl lays her eggs inside a big pile of leaves. As they rot, the leaves give off heat and keep the eggs nice and warm. Every day the father checks the nest with his beak. If it's too hot, he makes a hole to cool it down.

● Mockingbirds on the Galápagos Islands snatch hair from people's heads to line their nests.

Who lives in a city by the sea?

For many seabirds, a cliff is the perfect place to nest—it's out of reach for hunters, and handy for fishing. Thousands of birds lay their eggs on the narrow ledges or nest in cracks in the rocks. With all those birds fighting for space, it's like a city—crowded, smelly, and very noisy!

When do birds have teeth?

Inside the egg, a baby chick grows a little tooth on its beak. When the chick is ready to hatch, it uses this egg tooth to chip away at the eggshell from the inside. The baby bird never needs its tooth again, so it drops off soon after hatching.

● A kingfisher's nest is a stinking mess of fish bones and droppings. As soon as they leave the nest, the chicks dive into the river for a good bath!

1 A hatching bird chips a hole in the shell.

2 More holes make a dotted line.

Which eggs look like pebbles?

If you're walking on a pebbly beach in the spring, watch where you're putting your feet! Some of those round, speckly pebbles may be a plover's eggs. Plovers make their nests on open ground, but their eggs are perfectly hidden— because they look just like pebbles.

● Baby birds are hungry little things. A mother wren may feed her young hundreds of times a day!

Who starts life with a jump?

Mallard ducks often nest in holes in the trees, so their ducklings hatch high off the ground. How do they get down? Easy! When their mother calls, they jump out and tumble to the ground. They're so light that they don't need a parachute, and they all land safe and sound.

● Flamingo chicks feed on a runny food made by their parents. It's rather like mammals' milk—except that it's red, not white!

3 The end of the shell breaks away…

4 …and a damp duckling wriggles out.

5 Now the duckling is ready to explore.

● A duck egg hatches about four weeks after it has been laid. Hatching can take anywhere from an hour or two, to a whole day!

Why do geese take a winter vacation?

Brant geese fly from one home to another when the seasons change. This is called migration. The birds spend summer in the far north, feeding their chicks on grasses and other plants. But if they stayed for the winter, they'd starve! So each fall they fly back to warmer lands.

● It gets so cold in Antarctica that some penguins migrate northward to South America. They don't fly, of course—they swim!

How do they know when to go?

In the fall, the days grow cooler and shorter. This is a signal to migrating birds that it will soon be time to leave. They eat extra food, fattening themselves up for the journey ahead. Then on a fine day they gather together and fly away.

● The tiny rufous hummingbird spends the summer in Alaska and the winter in Mexico. That's a round trip of at least 6,000 miles!

How do they find their way?

Scientists aren't sure how migrating birds find their way. Some birds seem to know which way to go, as if they had a compass inside them. Others may steer by the Sun, Moon, and stars. Older birds may remember landmarks, such as rivers and hills.

● Flying long distances uses up a lot of energy. Weary birds stop off on the way to rest and fill up with food.

Which bird goes to sea?

The great wandering albatross spends most of its life at sea. This huge bird glides for hours on the wild ocean winds. Sometimes sailors see it following their ships across the southern seas.

Which birds walk on water?

When tiny storm petrels fish in the sea, they look as though they are walking on the water. They're not— they are actually fluttering just above the waves, paddling with their feet to steady themselves as they watch for fish below the surface.

Which bird wears a crash helmet?

Gannets are wonderful divers. They dive headfirst into the sea from a great height to catch their fishy dinner. But smacking into the water could give them a headache. That's why they have a thick, bony skull like a crash helmet, to protect them when they dive.

Who likes to wade in the mud?

Wading birds love the sticky mud at the mouth of a river. Huge flocks of them gather there to look for food, sticking in their beaks to hunt for worms, crabs, and crunchy shellfish.

● A puffin can carry home as many as 40 fish in its mouth. Little ridges along its beak give it an extra-firm grip.

How do penguins stand the cold?

The emperor penguin is the only animal to survive the Antarctic winter on land. Penguins have a thick coat of feathers, and an even thicker coat of fat under their skin. Even with their double overcoats, the birds huddle in huge crowds to keep warm in the biting winds.

● An emperor penguin chick snuggles between the legs of an adult penguin to keep warm.

● The snowy owl is a hardy bird. To keep out the Arctic chill, it has extra-thick feathers on its legs and feet—just like a warm pair of leggings.

● The ptarmigan lives in the far north. During the summer, its feathers are brown. But every fall it grows a new coat of white feathers—an excellent disguise to fool hunters in the snow.

● The male sandgrouse will fly hundreds of miles to a water hole to get a drink for his chicks. He soaks up water in his feathers, and lets the chicks suck it all out.

● In hot deserts, nesting birds have to shade their eggs from the sun. If they didn't, the eggs would cook, killing the young chicks inside.

How do desert birds stand the heat?

The tiny elf owl lives in the hot deserts of the Southwest. Like many other desert animals, it rests during the day, out of reach of the scorching sun. A nest hole in a saguaro cactus makes the perfect hiding place. The cactus's thick, juicy walls help to keep out the heat, making a cool shelter for a sleepy owl.

Why do people build nests for birds?

Some birds of prey are rare today because people once hunted them or destroyed their homes. So bird lovers are helping these birds to make a comeback by building nesting platforms in out-of-the-way places. As soon as the birds move in, people guard the nests so that the chicks can grow up in peace.

● Ospreys are fishing hawks that once nested in England, but not anymore. To encourage them to return, young birds are being moved from their nests in Scotland to new homes by an English lake.

● Every country has special groups of people who try to protect birds. Why not think about joining one?

30

- Oil tankers sometimes spill their oil at sea. When this happens, thousands of seabirds get covered in the stuff, and many of them die.

- In many countries people shoot birds for sport. Large flocks of migrating birds are easy targets, and thousands of them are shot every year. That's not fair!

Who dances with old feathers?

In Panama in Central America, hunters used to kill hundreds of rare macaws. They wanted their bright feathers for headdresses worn by traditional dancers. Today, zoos and bird-keepers all over the world save the feathers their parrots molt, and send them to Panama. The dancers wear those feathers—and the macaws in the wild keep theirs.

Index